AN ADOLESCENT'S CHRISTMAS: 1944

By Carol Bly

Changing the Bully Who Rules the World:
Reading and Thinking about Ethics

The Tomcat's Wife and Other Stories

The Passionate, Accurate Story

Soil and Survival (with Joe Paddock and Nancy Paddock)

Bad Government and Silly Literature

Backbone: Short Stories by Carol Bly

Letters from the Country

FORTHCOMING

My Lord Bag of Rice:
New and Selected Stories

AN ADOLESCENT'S CHRISTMAS: 1944

CAROL BLY

Afton Historical Society Press
Afton, Minnesota

Library of Congress Cataloging-in-Publication Data

Bly, Carol.
    An adolescent's Christmas: 1944 / Carol Bly. -- 1st ed.
      p. cm.
    ISBN 1-890434-18-3
    I. Bly, Carol--Childhood and youth. 2. Duluth (Minn.) Biography.
  3. Duluth (Minn.)--Social life and customs--20th century.
  4. Christmas--Minnesota--Duluth.   I. Title.
F614.D8B59 2000
977.6'771052'092--dc21   99-28414
                                              CIP

Printed in Canada.

The Afton Historical Society Press is a non-profit organization that takes pride and pleasure in publishing fine books on Minnesota subjects.

W. Duncan MacMillan   Patricia Condon Johnston
president   publisher

Afton Historical Society Press
P.O. Box 100
Afton, MN 55001
800-436-8443
email:aftonpress@aftonpress.com

Fifty copies
of the first edition of
An Adolescent's Christmas: 1944
have been numbered
and signed by the author
and handbound at
The Campbell-Logan Bindery
Minneapolis

This is the fourth annual
holiday book
published by the
Afton Historical Society Press

Earlier titles in this series:

UNDERGROUND CHRISTMAS
by Jon Hassler

FACES OF CHRISTMAS PAST
by Bill Holm

*CHRISTMAS AND NEW YEAR'S
ON THE MINNESOTA FRONTIER*
by Bertha Heilbron

This book is for Russell, John, and Malcolm McLean

TOLSTOY WAS TREMENDOUSLY MISTAKEN: happy families are unlike in their happiness. I feel a glad burst writing that blasphemy—*Tolstoy was tremendously mistaken*—like a child making a rude sign when at last the policeman turns his back.

A lifelong task of authors is to notice and engrave the ten or twelve percent dissenting opinion about anything that counts. If Tolstoy was simply wonderful, and he was, he must still have been ten or twelve percent mistaken about something—in this case about happiness in families. Authors' work is to honor some insights so peculiar that we are not sure it is all right even to harbor such thoughts. In this sense, authors keep on doing work that meditative adolescents start—harboring dissenting opinion, feeling uneasy about it, then trusting it for a time. Happy families are not alike, for example.

In my family the extroverts were courteous to the introverts! I especially noticed our family courtesy at Christmas, because Christmas is a season when outward-going people, at least in ordinary places like Duluth, Minnesota, most tend to be cruel to private people. In "A Christmas Carol," the nephew Fred doesn't complain about Scrooge's being tight-fisted at all: why should he? He is probably a Conservative himself—perhaps out of pocket, as Scrooge reminds him, but a Conservative. His morals are to do with family togetherness and a general affection for humankind. But how odd it is that Fred feels absolutely within his rights to insist that Scrooge be sociable—be talking and carrying on and eating in a large cheerful group. If Scrooge had been Goethe, that extroverted nephew would have tried just as hard to override the man's own temperament. "Forget all that about the *Gipfeln,* Uncle!" he would have cried, "Come stick with the rest of us on the low ground!" Or the Duluth parents of my old elementary-school friends: "Come down! come down!" these complacent extroverted parents had a way of shouting up the staircase.

"Don't skulk about in your room! It's Christmas! We want to be all together!"

But in my father's household no one used the phrase "skulk about in your room," and it was all right to do it. It was all right to skulk about for hours and hours of the Christmas holidays home from school, or in my youngest brother's case, home from Notre Dame where the Navy had sent him. In fact, that house, big, ill-afforded, what with our now dead mother's doctors' bills, was perfect for skulking about in. Our father did it himself. He never promoted sociability—except for this: we had to meet the formal occasion. He had a way of mustering us—the two children he had left home to muster. Step up to meet someone, he would say. Square your shoulders. Don't give adults such a handshake that they feel as if they've got hold of a dead mouse. Don't do it! he'd cry.

At five o'clock on Christmas Eve we would toast those who had left us and those now in danger, but we must stand up straight, please. Speak up clearly. Don't simper when we are toasting anyone, especially Mother. And don't grin. My widowed father liked form.

Covertly, he liked his office better than anywhere else, much as he loved the house. Even though his fourteen-year-old daughter had just got home from

Massachusetts, he wanted to return to his office. He half-disguised the longing. I told him I was happy to have him leave. I told him, I will bring down the crèche, Dad. I have homework to do, Dad.

Homework—not really—only Thomas Gray, "Elegy Written in a Country Church-Yard." This was the only poem I knew that plainly said it was just freak circumstance that Jews, Jehovah's Witnesses, Slavs, and other political prisoners were dying by the millions in Nazi camps and we were safe at ninety-two-and-a-half degrees of West longitude. I would memorize the poem.

My brothers and I came home from our schools in the 1940s on a Chicago and Northwestern Railroad train called The Duluth-Superior Ltd. It left Chicago in the afternoon, went all night through Wisconsin, paused in Superior, in the morning, and then came across the bay to Duluth at eight.

Our dad stood on the brick platform. He was always there, never late. He never wore his scarf high around his neck where it would do him any good: he kept his greatcoat collar down. White shirt-collar and foulard showed. He was fifty-seven, a big, hale man with a face red with cold. He had met us at Christmas so many times—all three boys from their schools and their colleges, and now, in 1944, me, and the next day, my youngest brother, that he knew exactly where the Pullman cars stopped.

Dad drove me slowly home through the cold morning. "There's your city," he would point out happily, a little loudly. "There she blows! There's the old aerial bridge! They may have good things at Abbot (or The Hill School or Asheville, as the case might be— this year it was my school, Abbot) but they haven't got the aerial bridge!" He was advertising Duluth to me, since I would be home for two weeks. He was advertising his life to me, to welcome me back home.

No one would salt the streets of Duluth for another two decades, so we drove on fair whiteness, handily, snow-tires creaking, my father brimming. We couldn't see them from where we were, but Dad reminded me that middle-aged men under his tutelage, the Temporary Coast Guard Reserve, were patrolling the docks and ways along the Harbor.

The deep motor of my own life got quieter and quieter. Now I was far from my boarding school, where people paid attention to an invisible part of me. I thought of my school as the car went along. I thought of the animal gentleness of that school, now that its mutterings and comfortable growlings were sinking away from me.

I felt the way you feel when you have been fathoming for something in deep lake water. You let down the weighted rope or netting, and for the fun of it, you imagine the deep water and whatever else might be down there. And next, you have the queer impression that what happens underwater is part and parcel of what happens in our medium, the air, and that you will never forget that part-and-parcelness, and will try all your life to keep your other thoughts connected with that impression, like an eider bird's nest, giving all the future insights you ever will have an invaluable warm surround. But you do forget. You forget fast as snow, and life strokes its way upward, back to the surface, secular as ever. Already in the car I felt that secularity joggling and grinning inside me as we drove along.

Here we were, then, going home—not many friends left here, but a few good ones. [What's a good friend? It is any girl who bothers to fix you up with a boy whose looks move you.]

Mother was dead two years now, but Dad was here and Malcolm was coming tomorrow. My elder two brothers were away at war but they were alive. Our father had had only the good kind of telegram. On behalf of the President of the United States, the Secretary of War wished to assure my father that his John was making a satisfactory recovery from appendicitis surgery at Anzio, and would soon rejoin his unit.

Cheer up then. None of us had been killed. Now it was snowing on the tongue-in-groove yellow streetcar, and the streetcar—beloved, howling type of transport—joined us from Wallace Avenue and was grinding itself along with us. Being in Duluth for Christmas, I said to myself as we passed Lewis Street, is enough for now. Like most adolescent people, I could do a quick-change mood act.

Still, I missed my absent life.

At fourteen I was a devoted writer of bad poetry. I framed up little sonnets, one after another, my three favorite subjects being the Gestapo, of whom I was terrified; Christmas, which I loved; and the war in the North Atlantic. My sources were, respectively, an issue of *Time* from three or four years before, my own life, and *March of Time* newsreels of destroyers attending troop convoys. I wrote pretty well on U-boats snaking along blackly in among our convoys. I didn't know anything one might do with *feeling* in a poem: I wasn't much interested. My idea was, state a point and get it right. I was willing to rewrite tirelessly. I forced my sturdy, dull ideas into the five-beat iambic line. Even though I was a fourteen-year-old girl, I had the love that old, educated, but unartistic males so often have: the love of sonnet writing. I preferred the Italian rhyme scheme to the Shakespearean.

At Abbot, my school, boarders had to be quiet from 4:40 to 5:20 in the afternoons and from 7:30 to 9:15 at night. I wrote my dull poems. "The Christmas bells are ringing once again," I wrote, then some other lines—then "something something is here once more——" then "something something something our brave men," and "Soon coming home from years of war." That last line being only four feet I needed another, so I handily added "and years" to the years I already had. "Soon coming home from years and years of war." New England seemed old, firm, and intellectual to me. I was glad enough to be home, but the school, the school, always the school, lay just under the skin of Christmas.

Our dad, glancing across Woodland Avenue, said, "There she is, waiting for the streetcar, to go to work as usual." He looked a little wistful. He always picked this neighbor up on the way to work. If he had been going downtown instead of home at this hour he would have picked her up. He gave her a tiny tank-commander wave. He would have talked some more. He gave me a covert glance, but I had a fourteen-year-old meanness about me. You would think I could at least ask him who she was. Adolescents are quite wonderful in their way, but they tend to be pigs too. I was too much a pig to let Dad fill me in on a fellow Duluthian, someone part of his daily life.

Finally home, Dad took my suitcases out and led the way up the basement steps from the garage. How much he wanted to return to his office to work! I would be left alone in the house. Was that all right?

He pointed out to me this year's tree. It was gigantic. The living room was fragrant with it. Dick had got it, good old Dick, Dad said, working ten, twelve hours a day now at the steel plant. Then he would stop trying to interest me in Dick's work in an Essential Industry: "Look here," Dad said, "Go through all *those* when you're settled in! Just have a look, dear!"

He was proud. We had got to the pantry. On the oak work surface, high so you could mix the drinks standing, were invitations to the annual Red Flannel Petticoats ball at the Kitchi Gammi Club, some other subscription dance at the country club, and a luxurious party at Margaret Culkin Banning's house. I was afraid of all those occasions. Dad read the invitations aloud though he had read them before. He kept pushing the cards toward me. "Not everybody gets invited to all that," he said.

You would think I could at least say, "You've done well, Dad. People like you. Look at what you've done for your children! Getting us invited to beautiful events!" I could have said that but perhaps fear made for meanness. Dances sometimes worked out all right, once in a while wonderfully, but often they didn't. Generally speaking, Duluth's family dances were a gravelly chore of the winter holiday.

"And the linen closet," our dad said, "I've got it all filled."

Our shabby towels lay folded, with the fold edges showing, and placed right at the shelf's front edge. Facecloths. Parthenon columns of toilet paper.

"We won't run out of anything," he said. If I found we needed anything, I should call him at the office, Melrose 6102, and he would buy it on the way home. He would bring home filets mignons for dinner, no worry about rationing stamps. He owned a hotel. Did I think we needed anything?

He longed for his office, for the usual day's work. Of course he did. And I loved him but longed for the empty house. "Dad, I will bring down the crèche and decorations."

He gave me a two-fold expression I would see a number of times on his face in later years. He couldn't quite make up his mind whether a daughter should be a Trophy Daughter, as we would call it now, or a daughter who should have *character* the way a son should. He had been able to study engineering for one year at the University of Minnesota. Then he had returned home to support his family. He became, at nineteen, an engineer, and was affectionately called "the boy contractor" by business people. He had the uneducated man's belief that people should work hard, but he also was wrapped in a fascination—a morbid fascination—for impractical subjects of study— English literature, for one. He was part and parcel of the philosophy that says if you study something lyrical and not visibly practical you are living an upper-class life. This was the British gentleman's principle of *waste* that exasperated Thorstein Veblen.[1] Throughout my childhood my father failed to encourage me to do work. The boys did the mowing. The boys carried firewood up from the basement. A girl was a girl, not a farm drone. He didn't know the passage in *Little Women* where Mrs. March took herself in hand and humbly applied to the servant, Hannah, to teach her the skills of housework. No one suggested I learn to cook. It is possible that my not learning women's work was a class dream of my father's.

Now my mother had been dead two years, however, and I was tall and strong. I had stumbled across the pleasure of physical work. I would bring the crèche down from the attic, with its Sea of Galilee and huge rocks symbolizing the mountains, the Taurus? or the Elburz?—that the three kings would have passed through.

At last my dad escaped, down the staircase, out the two-layered metal door to the garage.

I got downstairs with two very heavy rocks. Later the little stable and animals and Christ, Mary and Joseph, and the Magi. No one in Duluth but my family appeared to have rocks to their crèches—peaky, onerous, convincing. They were so sharp and heavy they cut my hands twice that Christmas, first coming down, then going back up.

Marie had once been live-in cook for my grandparents and parents. Now she loyally showed up to cook occasional dinners for my father. She cleaned the house regularly. I felt such a presence of *people in the background*—two brothers away at war, and the dead Jews mentioned in *Time*. A classmate at my school had had relations murdered in Germany. Once I heard a teacher saying this was a hard time for her—because of those relations in Germany. I heard this mentioned only once. Little was said about Germany, but what little was said went into me, just as some people learn a foreign language in a flash—as if they had always known it but had forgotten it. I had had nightmares about Germany for years, so no matter how thin my information about the camps, what Germans did lay viscous under everything, like dark scrim stuck under my Wright and Ditsons. It didn't get in my way, but it was always there.

In 1944 I didn't *know*, verbatim, that invisible people are real people and that every foreign policy affects invisible people in the world—either fairly or unfairly. I didn't know that, but I was coming to it, willing enough to skulk about my room during the holidays and think it over.

OUR FATHER POSTURED about the general shabbiness of our furniture, and our damaged roof. Like other people who had fallen into debt during the Depression and were now recouping during World War II, he was proud of paying old bills, one by one, two by two. When anyone said, Dad, we really ought to get a new living-room rug, he would remark, "I don't know! This one has stuck by us! What's wrong with our rug?" as if everything were a question of loyalty. As if the rug were an old milkcow who had a right, now she no longer gave milk, to take her ease in our pasture. If you pointed out what specifically was wrong with the rug, he would say, "Well, there are people who think they have to have new property all the time." Shallow people, clearly. If you decided to have it out—and not let him waylay you about holes in the rug or even more dire, the cracks in the roof—then he would suddenly, fast as a paperboy cutting through a private hedge, dodge into his favorite line of thought. "Funny thing," Dad told us, "funny how people who call themselves Christians have to have every new piece of furniture they see at Enger and Olson. Funny how of all people, churchgoers talk so Christian—but they live off the fat of the land!"

Well, there are social climbers. My father was awfully pleased at being a member of the Kitchi Gammi Club, but he was much less social climber than Moral Climber, if there is such a thing. Running down the property, letting the house roof leak—to him these were an ascetic virtue—abstention from living off the fat of the land.

For two years after our mother died in 1942, my three brothers carried down the tree lights and the rocks and the little stable with its wrapped figures. Then my oldest brother was commissioned and joined his ship at Bremerton. The next brother went to Camp Devon and Fort Bragg and Somewhere in North Africa. By 1944 he was Somewhere in France. The third joined the Navy's V-12, a college program, and thus could get home for Christmas of 1944.

Happy families are not only unlike in their behavior: they are unlike in their ideals. Even their few moral ideas differ, which is surprising because nothing is so like from one human being to any other as moral ideas. Everyone believes in hospitality. Everyone believes in fair play. Even thieves want the spoils divided up equally.

Yet some moral ideas are so spikey they pierce right up through the cloth of family and show. There is no point to pretending they don't. Duluthians showed us snapshots of their boy, dressed in cadet's dress white, a Firstyearman at Annapolis. "Like Kaiser Bill," our father said later. He said, in our family, we serve in wars when we are needed, but we don't go to college to become professional killers.

Annapolis and West Point turning out "professional killers"!

My mind leapt. Here is why: I was fourteen, a second-rate athlete carrying down from our attic the symbols of difficulties any magus must surmount or evade. I was struck whenever anyone, and this time it was my own father, said something no one else said. He was enacting a virtue not promoted by the Girl Scout leaders who sat dressed in silver-green around northern Minnesota campfires. They went on about the Great Spirit. What a relief it was to be fourteen, and not ten—to be free of the Great Spirit and to hear snappy judgments that divided one thing from another thing, even if they merely divided the U.S. Navy from the U.S. Naval Reserve.

I already daydreamed about young men—not much, only a little—I had only the most stringy expectations about sexual joy—but I daydreamed more often and more confidently, because my father openly disliked professional killing.

IN MOST HAPPY FAMILIES the extroverts shoulder the introverts this way and that way. The extroverts set the family style: they do the talking, and the talking is largely smiling and quickly turns ironical. "Oh is that so!" they exclaim. Kidding, lightly jeering, all in fun— in fact, fun itself—is the gross motor skill of most happy families. One can start kidding quite young. Kidding is by definition harmless: it is just kidding, but like a stream of water, it cuts its groove. I have heard people nearly on their deathbeds kidding someone.

Perhaps it has some use. Perhaps it steers the family values: jeering must be to families what clucking is to baby chicks. Go this way, not that way: think this, not that. Come here. Stay out of that! How else, unless the parents kid or jeer, unless the siblings kid one another, how else judge which ideas of the neighbors we should resist, which not, which of our own thoughts are sane and all right, and which are crazy and we had better not mention them to anyone.

Yet all the while, under this reindeer patter of kidding, one's inside mind longs for word of bad or sad news if there is any. One's inside mind is willing to be frighted by dreams—anything! Just any corroboration of serious news if serious news there is. Even Anne Frank wrote in her diary that although very privileged and happy, satisfied with her own charismatic good looks and her "darling" family, she could hardly bear "the endless round of jokes."

Our family erred on the side of grave little speeches. We gave a lot of little speeches to one another, small soundings-off on one subject or another. I suspect some echo of the memorial service hangs about like a fog around people who have had a death—the more so if they feel suspended between that death (in our case our mother's) and a present terror that one or both of the two older brothers might get hurt in the war. Perhaps we lounged in our rhetoric the way most Minnesota families use euphemisms. We never used the expression "if something should happen to . . ." We never used the phrase "pass away." But we were gassy. "If I should die, please destroy all the writing in my desk drawer without reading any of it," I told Malcolm. All right, he would. I believed him. I would never read anyone's papers without permission. Nor would he. [I was forty years old before I met what is apparently a common kind of person: mothers who equably go through their daughters' underwear drawers, knowing they will find secrets, and then reading the diaries they find.]

We were given to rhetoric in part for another reason: we were a drinking family. People who drink together, especially if they are often absent from one another, tend to talk seriously. Sometimes preposterously, but often not. Years later I rejoiced to read George Orwell's confession that it took him ages to leave off writing what was "mostly humbug." Humbug is a present comfort to the speaker, tight or sober.

The more admirable reason we took to rhetoric

was that we were so different from one another. Our father had come from a family that read the New Testament and some of Robert Burns aloud—little else, so far as we knew. Now that our mother had been gone two years, her cultural landmarks were beginning to vanish from the house. The musical scores for SATB voices disappeared from the the piano bench. I rescued the violin music, and still have it, but only she could play a stringed instrument. Our mother could read music, but the brother who took after her in this was in France this Christmas. I could only accompany our carol singing with three chords I had down pat—a major tonic, a dominant seventh, and the tonic chord based on the IVth note of the key. I could do just enough guesswork about diminished thirds to take us through the verses of "We Three Kings"—but what a relief to get to the refrain, which is major. I could only do even that much in the key of G which no one could sing very well.

This was a cultural vanishing. We scarcely noticed when it started—but in two years' passage no one could really remember any Dickens except to grin over drinks, and shout "Sam-avel, my boy" or at Christmas, "God bless us, every one!" No one could keep us steady through the French of the *Cantique de Noel.*

There was little we could do all together. I didn't play bridge and winter ruled out golf. We played Monopoly and Parcheesi with wit. We called people slum land-lords if they tried to make a killing off Baltic and Mediterranean. You were merciless if you kept renewing a blockade on your own Home safety.

We were better at abstract thought than art. Despite having had only one year of college, our father had as literary a mind as anyone I knew. He had three powerful tastes of literary people: he loved metaphor; he hated mealy-mouthed language; and he liked eternal, psychological truths. He especially liked it about death being that bourne from which no traveller returns since he didn't believe in an afterlife and considered people chicken—mindless—who did.

He kept us talking to each other. We had none of the surly silences towards parents so common in families with adolescent children. Mother was dead but we kept her present by talk, most of it sober. Dad's secretary sent us typed onionskins of our brothers' V-mails. He sent flimsies to each of us each week, mine the smeariest carbons because I was the youngest. He talked about the war a lot in these letters. He made sure we all knew that Ernie Pyle had spent a few days with John's outfit. He made sure that we knew that my brother Russell's job on the USS *Mississippi* was Damage Control. He made sure that my brothers knew I was a forward trying to make the varsity Gargoyle basketball team at Abbot.

Our family interest in World War II isolated us in a profound way from neighbors and a good many friends. Thousands and thousands of Minnesotans never heard anything about the concentration camps until they read Uris's *Exodus* years after the war. Thousands of girls my age had boyfriends in what they called "the service" without caring much which service.

I shall never be sorry that so much of our family talk was about affairs far away from our house and our city.

Though visiting distant relations thought we were a bunch of "drinkers" and we talked too much, we should have talked more, not less.

Our city, Duluth, had murdered two black people in 1920, but the *Duluth Herald* did not report it. I am afraid we congratulated ourselves a good deal on being good people. Our father and my brothers and I felt superior to American Southerners because we lived at the north edge of the country, right in the blasts coming down from Hudson's Bay—we congratulated ourselves just for coming from where we came from! It is amazing we didn't congratulate ourselves for breathing with noses instead of gills. We congratulated ourselves that although at various times family members had spent time in North Carolina, none of us slid to thinking that the routine 1940s cruelty of Southern whites to Negroes was all right.

I had a problem with corruption that Christmas. I wanted very much to please our father. It never occurred to me that I was being insincere in going along with some of the family rhetoric. I rarely lied and scorned any classmates caught cheating. But I sidled along with the social style of my family. I learned conventions. I asked the others to raise their glasses to some cause or other. Such drivel it seems now. Still, father, son, and daughter—we bolstered each other with our rhetoric, clumsily, amiably, like medical frauds who at least have a full-hearted bedside manner.

As I look backward at our Christmas of 1944, I feel more and more convinced that *family mention of horrible truths,* when those truths happen to be of great scope (such as genocide), is a great benefit to adolescent people. I emphasize "of great scope" because first, when two generations of a family talk about major evil together, intergenerational antagonism is less. They have some common cause. Second, talking about *evils of great scope* is especially useful for adolescents because they learn that some subjects are too great to trivialize. They learn some taste that keeps them from trivialization.

Here is a kind of trivialization of evil that got going, I am afraid, as an inadvertent result of the women's movement of the 1970s. Women got to saying things like, "Everything you do is a political act! When you grow a garden that is political." And "O yes, the Holocaust! Well, frankly, there's hardly a woman who hasn't experienced her own Holocaust!" We need Primo Levi, a writer especially bracing on the subject of not pretending one is standing up for some good cause when in fact all one is doing is planting flowers (or in Levi's case, mixing chemicals in labs). And since genocide by definition involves a *race* or genus being killed, it is both denial and grandiosity to claim you've experienced a genocide "in your own life." Such claims are half a question of tastelessness and half a question of making oneself be accurate. Introverts generally consider themselves more sensitive to other people's sufferings than extroverts, but they should learn, from extroverts, to be punctilious about data. We need to look at evil sensibly, then suggest changes in government. It is so much more important to *believe* in an evil than personally to *relate to* it.

I don't know from which field will come devotion and intelligence enough to interest everyone in stopping genocide. So far, outside of the serious genocide scholars like Israel Charny, Robert J. Lifton, and Eric Markusen, psychotherapy users and English departments do the most *talking* about "the holocaust." People write poems about Auschwitz or Wannsee. People write poems about Anne Frank. Some of the poems suggest that the poet is searching for *frisson,* or for seeming like a caring person, or for climbing on a bandwagon. Most of such poetry has struck me as moral fluff.

I hope that self-referencers from any movement and sensation-seekers among poets and memoirists do not become the arbiters on how we look at genocide and the bombing of whole cities. Kurt Vonnegut was rare in doing close onsite reporting without self-reference.[2] I am glad I was scared of the Gestapo although I never experienced the Gestapo. If I was scared at age ten, and stayed scared until age fourteen and even past it, it means that human beings can imagine what they will likely never see. It only sounds crazy to be scared of the Gestapo if you can't make yourself believe that what happens to people invisible to you really happens to them.

I value the shaky fears of adolescent people, therefore, more than I trust most sensitive fanfare on any subject.

WHAT IS A NEXT STEP after anyone has learnt about an evil?

My family was not so ignorant of European history as our neighbors were, but we acknowledged moral outrage only on the personal level, not as a passion that would make you want to change your government.

LET US SUPPOSE that moral outrage about national and international issues is a hardy skill, useful for one's psychological kit. At Notre Dame, my brother took courses appropriate for a future ensign. Neither the resident Roman Catholic instructors and professors nor the Navy officers on faculty assigned reading about the United States's closing its doors to further Jewish immigration from Germany in the late 1930s. I, too, was totally ignorant of any unpleasant news about my own country.

That ends up with my doing the glowing nightmares about Nazis, but not connecting it to my own country or my own life where I could work on them.

My father had been a drill sergeant in World

CAROL BLY

War I. In World War II, he was head of a temporary
civilian Coast Guard unit. To him moral life meant
being a responsible and altruistic family member.
When he entered the army in World War I, he wrote
out his paychecks before leaving for camp, each dated
with its month; he gave them to his mother so she could
cash them as fast as his soldier's pay would cover her
withdrawals. None of his civil-engineering textbooks
told him that the embassies of the Western powers knew
that the Turks were murdering the Armenians but
chose to do nothing. No one suggested to him that a
citizen of a democracy must occasionally criticize his
own government. A citizen should expect to start a
row if need be.

For the sake of *trying a hypothesis,* let us pretend
that my dad *had* heard of how we and the French and
the English and the Italians failed those Armenians.

Let us suppose that Dad would have had a great
many feelings about that subject. For example, might
he have felt something like the following feelings,
more or less in the order below? I am going to pretend
I am he, and make the list.

1. I wish no one had told me this. I love my

36

country and don't want it to have been that wrong with that *much* horrible result of its doing nothing.

2. Now that I know about the Turks' genocide, I feel angry. I am supposed to do something about it? None of my Presbyterian Sunday School teachers seem to be doing anything about it. No one else is. My new fiancee's family—agnostics, wits, social leaders, cheerful raisers of glasses to one cause or another—how bad do *they* feel about the Turks' genocide?

3. Well, if no one is talking about it, doesn't that mean there is nothing we can do about it? Isn't the only sensible thing is to realize: we can't win them all? The world has never been fair, after all: must I spoil my everyday good cheer because of the Armenians' being murdered?

(I guessed at the above because they are the responses I myself have still, in my late sixties, to any new anxiety or moral outrage that someone may wish on me.) To continue the hypothesis, then, about my father's feelings: after he had run through the above responses, he would pause and then possibly jump to No. 4 below. His (hypothetical) voice, again:

> 4. On the other hand, what if my consent-ing-to-hopelessness spreads like a flu going around and soon I will feel hopeless about issues closer to hand which I ought *not* to feel hopeless about? What if people never gave to charitable causes because poverty and illness look so hopeless?

Here he would have been brought up short. Mortal illness, like his wife's tuberculosis, responds wonderfully to research. Streptomycin had been worked up by the spring of 1942. Our mother had been given a dose, and for a moment her small claim to health had given a leap—but as it happened, her lungs were by then too far destroyed to hold. Still, our father knew that research on causes that outsiders blithely label "hopeless" costs money and it brings about cures.

All we had for psychological tools in 1944 was our family proclivity for serious talk.

We were a Republican family, but we were not cynics. We did not believe, as our neighbors did in their ambivalent but omnipresent cynicism, that

"Christmas is for kids." How cynical that is! How cynical it is to be a churchperson, and then coolly announce that Christmas is for little kids!

Radio brought a friendly kind of pop culture, some pleasant, some really dumb, right into the house. Our mother had been, and two of my brothers were, English majors so our house stayed as literary as we could keep it. No child ever sang "Santa Claus is Coming—to Town!" in our living room. I watched, in neighbors' houses, with morbid fascination, as little girls half my age wagged an index finger, rather sexily, for the lines "Better watch out! Better not pout!"

Our father made whole speeches of hatred for rikrak Christmases, the president of rikrak culture being Bing Crosby. Dad leapt out of his chair when Bing Crosby started to sing, syncopating "Silent Night" and scooping to the notes. Dad turned off the radio with a snarl. "To think that Mother had Christmas chorales here—and now this! Take that!"

Our father tended to announce his own opinions as if they were the opinions of all his children as well. He was kindly towards introverts, but a phalanx of unified opinion was what appealed to him.

"We don't believe in pretending there is an

afterlife," my father told us. "But Mother will be alive to us as long as we keep her alive in our hearts and minds." Then he added, being more moralist or drill sergeant than philosopher: "So that is what we're going to do. We are going to keep her alive in our minds." Like Dickinson, he saluted formality.

One way we kept our mother alive in our minds was to keep all her opinions going as well as we could. We loyally, albeit ridiculously, kept them going—even the unconscionable opinions. She had told us, for example, that the *Cantique de Noel,* and we called it that because *she* called it that—not "O Holy Night"—was in bad taste. But the tastelessness was lessened if you sang it in French instead of English. We sang it because Mother herself had typed up two French verses, adding the accents graves and aigues by hand to the copies. "Minuit, Chrétiens!" we sang, not one of us making a respectable asperate *R.*

We sang "O Tannenbaum" in German, pronouncing it any way we liked since it was only German. "O Tannenbaum" is a nearly perfect Christmas hymn. Of all the carols it is the most humble. It makes no claims to believing that Jesus is God or that I, singing this carol, am any more pious than I really am. It is a nature freak's carol and very beautiful. "O Christmas tree, you can make me very gratified!" That is so much more realistic a claim than "The hopes and fears of all the years / are met in thee tonight." Mother had written it out and Dad's secretary had made onionskin copies. Too bad we didn't learn "Es ist ein Ros' Entblumen," which is even more beautiful. To love a Christmas tree because it "blooms not only in summer but also in winter, what's more" is milktoast compared to the image of Christ as a rose in winter.

AT FOURTEEN I was like other adolescents who have learnt most of what they know at school, not home: I was happily "at-risk," as social workers now say, to feel the winter solstice. Herod's cruelty interested me. I couldn't get my opinions sorted out about such cruelty. I had no personal acquaintance who seemed likely to enjoy committing genocide like Herod.

I was no great shakes as a student in the 1940s, though I had a vague idea of spending hours and hours of Christmas vacation in a meditative study. My school had a handsome little magazine called *Courant*. I wanted with all my life's blood to be published in it. I felt religious, but it was difficult to write religious ideas when I was from an agnostic family. I didn't know how to *think* metaphorically. Since Jesus seldom spoke except in metaphor I didn't understand him.

But I vaguely loved him, in the same way that three years later, at seventeen, I would vaguely love Hamlet. In some spongy way I "identified with" both of them without the least understanding of their personalities. In fact, it never crossed my mind that Hamlet might have a personality quite opposite to mine. Just recently I found Harold Bloom's explanation of why so many people feel so close to Hamlet:

> In a lifetime of playgoing, one can encounter some samenesses among Lears, Othellos, and Macbeths. But every actor's Hamlet is almost absurdly different from all the others. The most memorable Hamlet that I have attended, John Gielgud's, caught the prince's charismatic nobility, but perhaps too much at the sacrifice of Hamlet's restless intellectuality. There will always be as many Hamlets as there are actors, directors, playgoers, readers, critics. Hazlitt uttered a more-than-Romantic truth in his: "It is we who are Hamlet.". . . Yet most of us are not imaginative speculators and creators, even if we share in an essentially literary culture (now dying in our universities, and perhaps soon enough everywhere). What seems

most universal about Hamlet is the quality
and graciousness of his mourning.[3]

I bring this up about projecting one's own fancies
on Jesus or on Hamlet, because such psychological
somersaults, which Jungians call "positive projections,"
help us keep clear of living fatuous or witless lives.
Anne Frank was seriously bored with "the endless
round of jokes," and *she* had read good literature and
presumably knew some history and the excitement of
math and geography. She and her family sang songs.
They knew words for songs. How much worse boredom,
then, American teenagers must experience now—
especially at Christmas, especially in the darkest days of
the year, when our minds most want to be serious!

Adolescents can hardly find a venue where even
the bravest person can say something solemn aloud.
No matter where they are—crowded into bright rooms
fragrant with pine or nowadays, sometimes, with pine
spray that you can jack into the sconce between its
candle and the backboard—how hard to say anything
that has not been said before! In most living rooms,
how hard it would be to remark, even if you kept the
tone casual: "Well—at least in some sense—Christmas
is not for children: it works best for adolescents!"

In any event, Christmas of 1944 suited me. I was darkly, secretly, happy the whole while. I had had to do some hard work in my head. I had survived some bruising failures. Classmates at my new school were better prepared than I. Their country-day schools had already made them at home with French, French pronounced impressively, and Latin, not just a vague stumble through the three-part Gaul with one's impedimenta, but serious selections from the Gallic Wars. A few had read Cicero and were starting Virgil. Worse than their superiority in coursework was these girls' knowing how to take notes in English and History classes. All I knew to do was to feel vaguely, improbably, moved, by much I heard.

My family divided up family style into culture and non-culture. Please be cultured, O! please be cultured! our house seemed to grunt. Wagner yes, Mozart yes, Jingle Bells no, Up on the House Top no. We were for culture. Now Abbot, the school, forcefully showed me that some cultural ideas are more complex and therefore more valuable than other cultural ideas. A scholar must practice discernment between what was facile or immoral on the one hand, and what was complex and philosophically *good* on the other. One of my classmates, herself only fourteen, announced that of course she loathed Wagner. I was brought up short. I had done nothing more discerning that to pit my dead Mother's Wagner against the neighbors' "Up on the House Top!" For the first time in my life I asked myself, "Am I comparatively stupid?"

That painful question helped me jump up into the mindset that divides adolescents from children: I could hold opposite feelings at the same time. I had lost my intellectual confidence, but at the same time did not really feel stupid so much as nutty and rapt where others were easy. I had as much feeling as others. I knew how to make my mind turn over and over two apparently contradictory insights at the same time. A quarter-century later I came across Tolstoy's description of the general who seemed dazed to his younger staff officers. How would they save Moscow? That was their question. The young officers came up with battle plan after battle plan. The old man said nothing. He is losing it, they thought. Then one day he told them what they would do: they would not fight to save Moscow at all. They would retreat to east of Moscow, let Napoleon take the city, and then, and *then,* they would fight. The officers shrieked at him. Let the French take holy Moscow! But he had finally weighed everything. If they fought to save Moscow, their army would be ruined and they would lose Russia. If the French were let into Moscow, the Russians would gather themselves and when they were ready they would drive the enemy not only out of Moscow but out of Russia.

Until I read that passage I didn't understand something that adolescents sooner or later must undertake: they should weigh everything about what to do, all the pros and cons they can. They should take their time. They should keep conflicting evidence in hand—peacefully keep conflicting evidence in hand, as if each piece of information were a junior officer in your organization. Take time.

This winter of 1944 I allowed myself to relax and be on both sides of several issues. I was stupid or I was not. There was something mysterious and worthy in me, as in others, or there was not. I wrote my mediocre poems for hours and hours. I knew it was mediocre to change the meaning of a poem so that the a b b a and c d d e, and worse, even the wrap-up, the f g h, f g h rhyme scheme came out right. Or to change a poem so that the processions of *U*s and slashes stretched each line to 5 beats. I also knew that a fine cave lay under my brains sending up utter happiness.

I learned not to mention utter happiness to relations. One mustn't make demands on them. One had better not talk about feeling utterly happy just as one had better not tell relations that you have nightmares about Nazi Germany.

A half century later we would have called it "inappropriate self-revelation" if someone stood in the Hunter's Park Post Office in Duluth, buying high-denomination stamps, and suddenly said, "I am buying a lot of these high-denomination stamps because my mother always kept them, along with the family stationery, in the living-room desk. This is one way I am keeping alive the world as it was when she was living in it."

The postmaster looked first shocked, then disagreeable, then vapid.

I learned an adolescent's Christmas lesson: wait out Christmas vacation. Keep your mind on *sensuous* life, not *thinking* life. A friend was going to fix me up with a boy for a basement rumpus-room party. I meant to arrange the crèche, keep some of my mother's traditions going, kiss that boy in the rumpus room if he was the same one I thought he was. In January I would go back to the monastic life.

I would lie, of course, as needed. Once you put on an evening dress, you may as well be a nice girl and say things people want to hear. At the Red Flannel

Petticoats dance, old men, thirty-eight or thirty-nine if they were a day, asked my father's daughter to dance. Everything was family. We danced with each other's parents and children. One or another said, "How do you like Abbot?"

If you are not from a small city like Duluth, you may not know that in a wartime city of 101,065 people, a few parents knock themselves out to send adolescent children to serious schools. We would see one another on the brick platform of the Chicago and Northwestern Railroad, the waiting parents' cold faces kissing our faces hot from the train. These parents were very interested in one another's children at Christmas. Schooling—where you did it, whether it worked out, how in the world to get it all paid for— all that was of passionate interest to all generations.

Old man in white tie, waltzing very fast and beautifully. He said, "Well, how's Abbot?" because it had been decades since his own schooling.

"Fine!" I exclaimed. Waltzing allows only exclamations.

"Great kids!" I added.

Dance partner: "How're the teachers? I had some terrible masters at the Hill."

Give a face. "Bunch of bags!" I exclaimed, and

the partner laughs, "Yes, that's what our E.J. says about the Dobbs people! Bunch of old bags!"

"Frustrated old bags!" Dance partner throws his head back and laughs at this. Thus I lightly sold out my mentors. "Frustrated," in 1944, meant only sexual deprivation: its present use as a mild form of anger or feelings of workplace helplessness didn't come in until the 1960s.

Someone cuts in. A boy.

Another man, then, loyal friend of Dad's. Two boys. Then my brother, too, watching, making sure I am having a good time. I often don't at a dance, but tonight I do. Still, he is checking.

Another father. "How's Abbot? We've got Buffs going to Dana Hall, and she's liking it!"

I don't like Buffs. She is what is called a popular kid. She never has a bad dance, and therefore is a shallow, greedy, stuffy, apple-polishing beast. I tell her father, "The social life at Abbot is terrific!" so she gets that news of me. That's right, he remembers conversationally: you're the people with the campus right next to Andover!

"Such as it is," I say in a wise, vapid tone, adequate for foxtrot.

Then at New Year's—a rumpus-room party.

How curious it was to kiss that boy over and over. Great luck, too—the boy *was* the one my friend had tried to describe. People complain of how teenagers talk inchoately now. It was quite bad even in the 1940s. "This boy," she said, advertising him to me, "was like tall, and he had like dark hair and bedroom eyes." The word "like," already in the predicate of sentences, would not make it to the *front* of the sentences until the Bay Area of 1969 or 1970. In 1970 she would say, "Like you'll really get into this guy."

This boy had sweet lips. I later met only two men all my life who had that particular quality—sweet lips. Such men weren't necessarily the most stirring kissers, but they were the sweetest. You lingered without shame. Men who give sweet kisses have this about them: you needn't do any intellectual work about those fellows. You needn't try to get a line on whether they have any character or not. Their *selves* really don't matter at all. You just trust the kissing. As soon as you kiss someone like that you know that kissing is a very good place, and you should stay in it, and not make inquiries.

ON THE SECOND DAY of the New Year, my father and brother had gone down to the family office for a few hours. I lay under the drying tree, glad to be alone. I had no models of people who liked to be alone. What if all girls and women want to be alone a good deal more than we allow for? Buddhists and Christians and great half-alienated authors like Pär Lagerkvist and Thorstein Veblen and William Hazlitt want to be alone, but who says it is all right for women and girls to want solitude? I felt wrong-headed about it. At fourteen I had already started the particular kind of emotional waste which is feeling wrong-headed for wanting solemnity. I was waking up to life as a thinking person all right—yet even as I was waking I began to waste my mind.

Nineteen forty-four was an easy time for us who weren't at the Battle of the Bulge or Leyte Gulf. I didn't know America's ethical intellectuals like Dwight Macdonald and Norman Cousins. I had not even read Thorstein Veblen. Though I had been assigned *A Room of One's Own* and I had read it through, I hadn't the least idea what Virginia Woolf was getting at. I hadn't the tiniest inkling of what it means to want *reform*. I had never met anyone who intended to change the world. The best I knew of were people who wanted to keep the Duluth Symphony going.

Therefore, morally scant, but curious, my conscious mind, and the conscious minds of my acquaintance, trotted about their little paddocks more easily than anyone's mind can now. We liked Ike and eight years later would say so. We didn't know he worried about a military-industrial complex. We didn't imagine that in the next few years rich advertisers would dominate American living rooms with sights and sounds of murder, hour in, hour out, because violence fascinates ill-educated people, and people habituated to fascination like fascination better than thinking and they buy products more readily than thinkers do. We knew no group psychology. We could not have guessed that critically massed rich men, once they sit in meetings together, apparently can't control their own behavior: they can't make themselves stand up against what is wrong. If a little task force of two or three come to a meeting, reporting after months of committee work, and make their proposal, the others apparently can't make themselves speak up against it. Irving Janis had not yet done his amazing book about "groupthink." In 1944 I didn't have to ask myself, "Can't privileged adults in their alpha dens make themselves stop doing wrong?" Adolescents suffer more now. Psychological research reports that the second cause of suicide in American adolescents is ethical anxiety: the young people don't think their elders, their leaders, will keep them safe.

I did what I could at fourteen. I had bad dreams about Nazi cruelty. I lied about having such dreams, but I didn't deny them.

THE GENERAL READING audience—educated people not specialized in some one scholarly field—are usually about forty years behind in the news about any given science. People, especially in eastern America, still think you go to a psychiatrist if you are disturbed; they don't know you go to a psychotherapist to deepen consciousness. Learning to recognize and then respect—not disdain—psychological dynamics is still undreamt of, as Hamlet would say, in the philosophies of privileged, educated Easterners. Even Freud's work wasn't talked about in the 1940s or even 1950s at the Kitchi Gammi Club in Duluth, although Kitchi members, especially the college-graduate women among them, stayed on top of *The New York Times Book Review* and took the trouble to stay current with political news. I had moved from Duluth before the 1960s or 1970s, when the scholarly and the half-assed and the outright crazy books stemming from C.G. Jung's ideas swept across the United States. I have the impression that Jungianism never cut the wide swath with Duluth intellectuals that it cut with so many New York, San Francisco, and Twin Cities intellectuals. Now that Jungianism has ebbed, probably Duluth's intellectual ambiance is like a landscape that escapes the glaciation that has flowed and scraped around it: its surface remains untouched from forces that were cataclysmic for so many others.

Since it is possible for entire forcefields to go past unnoticed, we ought to ask ourselves: now, in 1999 and 2000, what is going on that conventionally educated people are uninformed about?

Two answers: the new neuroscientific researches and dynamic-systems thinking. This decade's news about how our minds work is absolutely wonderful. It gives hope. It returns to us, after so much philosophical and lab-style determinism, interest and confidence in our own wills. The researches being reported now are a thousand times more elegant and intricate than the left-brain/right-brain chatter of twenty years ago.

I am going to describe only one premise. This premise underlies new thinking in both neurobiology and dynamic-systems theories of development. Forget the old dichotomies—nature versus nurture, heredity versus environment, background versus experience, and so forth.

This premise says: everything there is, from cells to brains to the organism we call a human being, creates itself by its very functioning. The mind makes itself as it goes along. Example: the moment a mind decides outright—using words to itself—that it doesn't believe some doctrine it has been told all its life, it becomes a mind with a new habit. That new habit is the habit of asking, "Well, if such and such a particular doctrine is *not* true, then what might be true?" That mind is no longer the same mind it was a moment ago because now its neurons are touching around, lighting up groups of other neurons, checking back, all that skinny fire darting about and branching to other skinny fires, questioning everywhere: do we believe this? are we afraid? are we excited? shall we explore? shall we try *this* hypothesis? is some of what we thought true a lie? how much of it is a lie? should I be frightened or should I be curious? All those kinds of questions change the mind each millisecond. The mind of a follower, never having done such questioning, hasn't yet become the kit of leadership.

According to dynamic principles, transitions to new forms involve the loss of stability, so that systems can seek new, self-organized patterns.[4]

Loss of stability! How terrifying that is! A follower's mind hates to contemplate loss of stability. Yet a brave "self-organized" mind may two seconds ago have been only a follower-mind. This is near the very center of dynamic systems theory. To change, to become ethically complex, you must lose stability. Well, that is an idea that has been dear to liberal-arts educators ever since Epictetus. Wooden-headed people seriously hate it.

A cheering side-benefit of dynamic-systems theory is that it gives us some hints about how to encourage adolescent people. "I never heard that before!" we can shout, after our teenager has spoken. "Where did you pick up on such a terrific idea anyhow? Say more! I have to think about this. You may be wrong. In fact, I half-hate the sound of what you're saying—yet, yet, you may be onto something so right that it will *change* some things!"

We won't be praising young people in order to help them clarify their new philosophies. They will in fact get clear better without us. We are praising their new idea because their having come out with any new idea at all means they have jumped electrically and vaulted new connections in their brains. Their brains have become one step more "self-organized." We want to welcome adolescents to the life of thinking, jerky, unsure, nutty, numinous as it is. We want them to run through these new connections some more. We want them to connect these new connections exponentially with still other, newer connections. If we love them, we want young people to be every minute more self-organized.

If we ourselves, however, are so afraid that we cannot abide instability, we may remark, as wooden parents do, "Listen, wherever this new rot has come from, I don't want to hear it again, not in this house, not from any kid of mine." The kid may then back off from that flaring new life of the brain. Then the brain, always *becoming* as it *functions,* simply pulls out of those new circuits just the way you can pull a cord or two out of the Christmas tree lighting and make it shorter. From now on it will be a brain without those tentative new branch-circuits.

We could break the pattern of educated, reading kinds of people always being forty years behind in new thinking. I think it a pity that people are stuck on left-brain/right-brain pronouncements when they could be reading Gerald Edelman's *Bright Air, Brilliant Fire* and *A Dynamic Systems Approach to the Development of Cognition and Action* by Esther Thelen and Linda Smith. These books are inviting. They give us ideas on how we can help turn the nascent dreams of adolescence into pro-activism.

I am going to make up an example. The example will be myself, in Christmas of 1944. This adolescent person has the horrors about genocide, the Nazi genocides. This person has bad dreams. This person also, however, has an affectionate family who are all feeling bruised from the mother's death. This family is hoping the two older boys will come home safe from France and the Pacific. This family wouldn't want to hear that the adolescent is having bad dreams. Please just go to dances, or if you like, write sonnets, they would say. Please be happy. Come play Monopoly. This affectionate and basically happy family have what Thelen and Smith call strong "attractors" to keep things as they have been in the past.

The adolescent has strong "attractors" to change, however. One task of all adolescent people is to be respectful of their own attractors to change. Adolescents *need to become unstable.* They need to be willing to weigh opposites, willing to drop authority, and willing to become and stay "self-organized." Jesus was right that it is hurtful to leave behind your parents' homey, conservative philosophies. It takes a sword, he said, using metaphor.

The sword can sometimes be just some new information. How helpful it would have been if my family or anyone I danced with or my friends had read dynamic-systems theory! If Thelen and Smith's book had existed back then and had lain with *Time* on my father's table and I had read it, I might have recognized my own dilemma. I might have refused to waste my personality the way girls and women of the 1940s were pressed to do.

I may have had strong "attractors to change," but I was also still half-trying to keep Christmas as it was when our mother was alive. I admired her for having kept house letterhead in a black walnut desk in the living room. You could tell she wanted people to write letters there, like the Englishwomen in Daphne du Maurier. (They vanished into the Morning Room to write letters. Higgins, I shan't want to be disturbed, but do bring morning tea at eleven if you'd be so kind.)

Mother's stationery said only "2400 Butte Avenue, Duluth, Minnesota." In 1944 postal zone numbers were still in the future. I meant to get more stationery printed. I got more stamps, not just 3s, but a spread of denominations, so you could see this was a living, properly equipped household, with a serious, writing woman keeping track of things. I wanted my brother and me to write our Christmas thank-you letters at that desk.

In the basement laundry room I found a loyal maid's mending. Marie had collected my father's holey socks and piled them, with a darning knob, in a brown basket. Well, I would mend them. If Marie was so faithful that she came regularly to keep our house clean and to mend, I would do it, too.

On January 2 it was time to take the crèche and the animals and heavy rocks back up to the attic. I, too, could mucilage labels in upper-and lower-case wide-nib printing onto the boxes. Here is the stable. Here are the manger and the smaller figures. Here is the Sea of Galilee. Here are the mountains with their bleak passes.

After wasting a few hours I let the desk alone. I darned one sock. I decided that what looked like sloth, and ninety percent was sloth, kept me from finishing the darning. Ten percent of my quitting was a new idea, however: this house was no longer a home with a mother in it. This house would not be my home much longer.

Someday I might label boxes carefully and sing Christmas cantatas in German and keep family socks darned, but I wouldn't be doing it here, period.

But in the meantime! in the meantime, I told myself—I was going fast as falling into a valley—the mind is real. The mind is not a glassy reservoir of culture. If our mind gets focused on some bad thing, like people torturing other people—if our mind uncloaks that subject again and again in its dreams, it means our mind wants to change that one bad thing. We had better give our mind respect. We had better not shake hands with our mind so weakly that our mind thinks it's got hold of a dead mouse.

And another thing—I was winding down now, but still going fast: about the Magi and camels and the ominous mountains: T.S. Eliot was right. It is one thing for animals to whine when they are galled or sorefooted and keep trying to lie down in the snow. It isn't anywhere near good enough for people.

NOTES

1. Thorstein Veblen, *The Theory of the Leisure Class*. Veblen was even more explicit in *The German Empire* about privilege showing itself by how much it simply wasted.

2. Vonnegut was a prisoner of war at Dresden.

3. Harold Bloom, *Shakespeare: The Invention of the Human*, New York: Riverhead Books, 1998, p. 413

4. Wapner and Derrick, *Dynamic Systems Theories*, Thelen, E. and Smith, Linda B., p. 601

Carol Bly was born in Duluth and educated at Abbot Academy, Wellesley College, and the University of Minnesota. She has written several books of essays and short stories. Her most recent publications are *Changing the Bully Who Rules the World* (Milkweed Editions, 1996) and "Chuck's Money" (*TriQuarterly*, May 1999). Forthcoming works include *My Lord Bag of Rice: New and Selected Stories* (Milkweed Editions, 2000) and a book on new ways to learn and teach creative writing (Anchor, 2001). She is presently the 1998–99 Edelstein-Keller Author of Distinction at the University of Minnesota.

Two of Carol's three brothers mentioned in this book—Russell and Malcolm McLean—live in Minnesota. John McLean lives in Tucson. At the time of *An Adolescent's Christmas* (1944), Russell McLean was a lieutenant (j.g.) on the USS *Mississippi*; John McLean was a Private First Class in the 160th Field Artillery Battalion of the 45th Infantry Division; and Malcolm McLean was a midshipman at Notre Dame University, in the Navy's V-12 program.

Carol Bly lives in St. Paul. She is the mother of Mary, Bridget, Noah, and Micah Bly.

Designed by
Mary Sue Englund
Nashville, TN

Typeface is
A Garamond